# Dinosaur

Meredith Hooper

Illustrated by Bert Kitchen

This book is about plant-eating dinosaurs called maiasaurs.

CAMBRIDGE
UNIVERSITY PRESS

# Maiasaurs were middle-sized dinosaurs.

Maiasaurs were up to 9 metres long –
that is as long as two of today's biggest
crocodiles. They weighed 2 tonnes –
that is as heavy as four crocodiles.

They lived in huge herds.

Tyrannosaurs hunted maiasaurs, so it was safer for maiasaurs to stay together.
    When maiasaurs needed to move quickly, they ran on their strong back legs. They used all four legs when they walked along slowly.

Maiasaurs made their nests out of mud and pebbles.

Every year, a herd of maiasaurs walked to a dusty plain by a lake. Here they made their nests and laid their eggs. The nesting place was very crowded, noisy and smelly. There was just room for a maiasaur to stand between one nest and the next.

Each mother maiasaur laid about twenty-four eggs in her nest.

Maiasaurs put sand and plants on top of their nests to keep the eggs warm and dry.

There was a space between each egg so that the maiasaur hatchlings could break out of their shells easily.

After the young maiasaurs hatched, they stayed in their nest.

Maiasaur hatchlings came out of their eggs looking very like their parents, but they were twenty-five times smaller and two thousand times lighter.

The hatchlings stayed in their nest for about sixty days.

Some kinds of dinosaurs ran around as soon as they came out of their eggs. Maiasaurs hatched with weak bones, so they were helpless and had to be looked after by their parents.

# Maiasaurs ate a lot of leaves and plants.

The maiasaurs quickly ate up all the plants near the nests. The young maiasaurs were hungry and they needed to grow fast.

Every day, the parents carried food to their hatchlings.

The parents worked hard bringing food to the nest. They had to walk further and further to find more food.

Troodonts were meat-eaters.
They hunted young maiasaurs.

Troodonts ran very fast. They had big eyes and big brains.
They had teeth which were very good at grabbing, and hands
which could hold things. They had a curving claw on each
back foot. Troodonts could rip things apart with one kick.

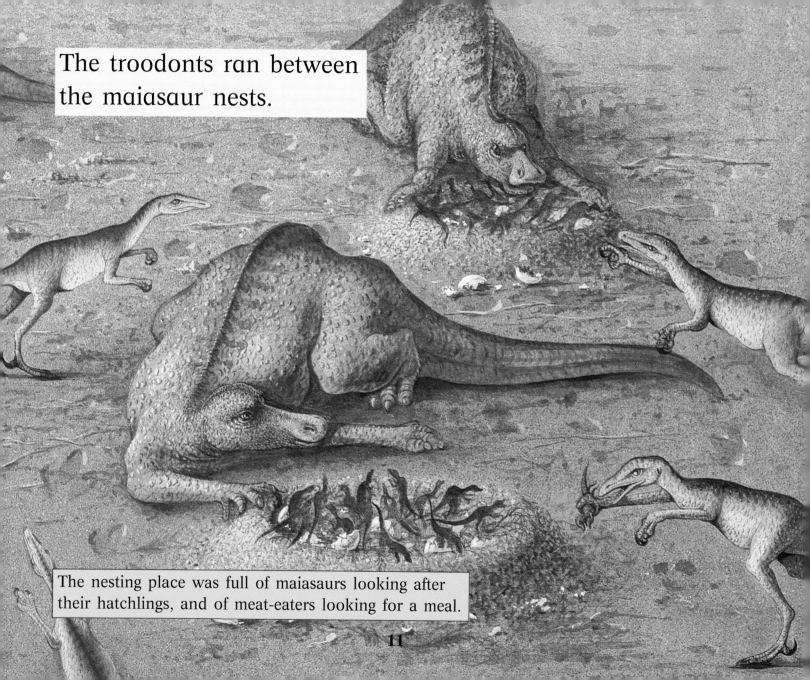

The troodonts ran between the maiasaur nests.

The nesting place was full of maiasaurs looking after their hatchlings, and of meat-eaters looking for a meal.

chasmosaur

As soon as the young maiasaurs were strong enough, the maiasaur herd left the nesting place. The maiasaurs needed to find more food.

pterosaur

ankylosaur

tyrannosaur

13

This is the
size of
a maiasaur
egg.

A maiasaur egg weighed
1.2 kilograms (1,200
grams).

A one-day-old maiasaur looked like this.

A young maiasaur weighed
1 kilogram (1,000 grams)
when it hatched. When it
was one day old, it was
35 centimetres long.

The maiasaurs in this book lived 75 million years ago in what is now the state of Montana, USA.

Fossilised maiasaur nests have been found just where they were built. Inside the nests are fossils of eggs, pieces of egg shell, baby maiasaurs and bits of the food that they ate. There are also fossilised troodont teeth.